I0558535

UNTOILING
OF A
WOMAN

Love Letter to the Father

UNTOILING
OF A
WOMAN

Love Letter to the Father

L.T. SIMMONS

ARPress

Copyright © 2024 by L. T. Simmons

All rights reserved. No part of this publication may be reproduced, distributed, or transmitted in any form or by any means, including photocopying, recording, or other electronic or mechanical methods, without the prior written permission of the copyright owner and the publisher, except in the case of brief quotations embodied in critical reviews and certain other noncommercial uses permitted by copyright law. For permission requests, write to the publisher, addressed "Attention: Permissions Coordinator," at the address below.

ARPress
45 Dan Road Suite 5
Canton, MA 02021

Hotline: 1(888) 821-0229
Fax: 1(508) 545-7580

Ordering Information:
Quantity sales. Special discounts are available on quantity purchases by corporations, associations, and others. For details, contact the publisher at the address above.

Printed in the United States of America.

ISBN-13: Softcover   979-8-89330-328-5
          eBook   979-8-89330-329-2

Library of Congress Control Number: 2024901007

CONTENTS

DEDICATION

Birthed out of a time of fasting and praying between women who just want HIS face!

Continually, I say, "The Lord be magnified who takes pleasure in prospering Mommie, Sister Gloria, Sister Ann and Sister Pam!"

PROLOGUE

If you love Me, show it by
doing what I've told you

—John 14:15

You have exalted above
all else Your name and
Your Word and You have
magnified Your Word above
all Your name!

—Psalm 138: 2b

First, I considered the Centurion's
faith in the self-fulfilling power of
the spoken Word by the Lord Jesus to
save the life of his servant. Secondly, I

considered that the Lord Himself was well pleased with the man's trust, reliance and dependency on the ability of the Word to perform by its own virtue.

The Word of God is power to undo and reverse any toil, any wrong, any injustice and anything we deem unsavory, contrary or illegal in our lives. The Everlasting Father has given to those who believe power with a mandate assuring us in the Book of John that if we steadfastly believe in Him, we will be able to do the same things He did; and we will do even greater things because He went to the Father. He did not say these words to pass the time nor to fill up space as if having an awkward moment! The words that He speaks, they are spirit & they are life. Moreover, He is too Divinely smooth to have an awkward moment!

So why make such a decree? Ladies, this is a command to do what He has told us to do, a spirit-filled example for us to see how He does things and then to show how much we love Him by doing what He did! For the Centurion who had a tragic personal circumstance, Jesus spoke the Word only because the man believed that the Word would undo and reverse the distress in his home. Unlike the Centurion, we have the living Word of God, ripe and ready to put in our own mouths to declare and decree a thing! In this, we are already doing greater things! To live the best life from the inside out, we must agree with the Holy Spirit Who saw it fitting to inspire the recording of the words of the Centurion, speak the Word only!

L.T. Simmons

April 2011

LOVE LETTER TO THE FATHER

Lord, YOU truly are the Most High God, the King of kings, the King of glory, the King of majesty…YOU ROCK & YOU RULE!

Lord, I start out undone. I'm coming to the throne of grace of a HOLY, HOLY, HOLY God! Seeking the face of God from the perspective of JESUS CHRIST as best I know how, with the help of the Holy Spirit. Father, forgive me for many words, for it is not my intent to be a clashing symbol. But when I sit and be still, I'm blessed to come to know that YOU are God & there is still more God for me to know. I humble myself before YOU casting my cares and anxieties on YOU, once and for all, because I know YOU care for me & that which concerns me watchfully & affectionately.

By CHRIST JESUS, I am the righteousness of GOD! So I declare that I am always in the right place at the right time…in right standing with God…having a pure heart toward HIM. I am driven by the Kingdom of God first! I am a giver, giving as I purpose in my heart & I am a cheerful giver. God loves me & because HE is able, He is making all grace abound toward me today. So, I always have all sufficiency in all things so that I have abundance for every good work in the Kingdom of God, dispersing & lending at home, abroad & to the poor.

Lord, always keep my heart, mind & eyes open that I may see & receive YOUR TRUTH.

Father, YOU supply seed to the sower & bread for food. So, Father, I thank YOU that YOU supply & multiply that seed I have sown & increase the fruit of my righteousness.

Isaiah 55:8-11 says that, As the rain comes down & snow from heaven and do not return there, but water the earth and make it bring forth & bud that it may give seed to the sower & bread to the eater, Lord YOU said, "So shall MY word be that goes forth from MY mouth; it shall not return to ME void but it shall accomplish what I please & it shall prosper in the thing for which I sent it. ****Revelation! Revelation! Revelation!

Father God in Heaven, thank YOU, for giving understanding on this WORD from Isaiah 55:8-11. With the Holy Spirit's help, the meaning of this Word has come to life. The rain & snow come down from heaven, just like the Words from YOUR mouth, therefore they come with force, power & authority <u>to make</u> things happen, to change things from one state of being to another! Where things were once dead, it can now produce, bring forth & bud! Because of YOUR goodness, the bud won't come forth empty, but it contains seed in it for the due season. The sower & the eater can have bread! I see that YOUR Word tells me that the bud "may" give seed to the sower. "May" indicates room for choice, decision & effort on the part of the potential sower. Father I chose the seed so that I can have bread to eat and so that my heart can be strengthened at any given time!

Father, I am grateful that YOU assure me further that not only will YOUR Word come forth with substance, but it will do two things: #1 It will accomplish what YOU please. Faith pleases YOU. So, every time I take YOU at YOUR Word by faith, stand on it & speak it myself, I will see the marvelous results of what it accomplishes in my life! #2 YOUR Word will prosper in the thing for which YOU sent it. The Lord be magnified Who takes pleasure in the prosperity of His daughter!

Thank YOU Lord that YOU are helping me to see that when I speak YOUR word it is giving voice to YOUR word & the angels hearken to it to do the Word for me!

Praise YOU that YOU have delegated to us, have birthed in us, have wrapped us up in & have wrapped up in us RAW SUPERNATURAL POWER in the Person of the Holy Spirit Who hovers, BUT THEN when the Word of God is pronounced, HE MOVES in us, for us & through us to renovate the very ground we walk on to the point that <u>truly we are blessed</u> going in & out, in the city & the field, full baskets & vats, Only Above & never beneath, Goodness & Mercy are in Hot Pursuit of us all the days of our lives, no need for a want, no weapon formed against us shall prosper…in a WORD, FAVOR FOR LIFE!

Lord, thank YOU for being so very able & faithful to give YOUR children grace with revelation in our time of need. I believe that even one revelation has already brought a revolution & changing the situations in my life & in the lives of those around me. So, Father, with a heart of gratitude regardless of the situation, I will Praise YOU Lord my God & I will give YOU thanks for the little things. Just like Jesus gave thanks when the "dinner for one" of 2 fish & five loaves of bread were all that were presented to Him in the midst of thousands of mouths to feed. YOU still showed Yourself faithful and MULTIPLIED THAT SEED that was sown, HALLELUJAH! YOU have & are still taking me/us to a higher level of saying, thinking & therefore living this abundant life that the Lord JESUS CHRIST came to give us, paid the price for & shed His Precious Blood for.

Lord, YOU are no respecter of persons but YOU look at the heart. Search me & know my heart, test me and know my anxious thoughts & lead me in the way everlasting! I choose to abide in YOU Lord Jesus. Thank YOU for abiding in me by YOUR spirit & life-WORDS in me so that in this intimate more than real communion with You, I bear much fruit. I have the right to ask what I desire and it shall be (and is even being done) for me (now). By this, OUR beautiful, wonderful heavenly Father is glorified! Lord I trust YOU & I follow YOU! Whatever YOU tell me to do, I will do, so that my transformation is sure to manifest.

Lord, with the help of the HELPER Who is the Holy Spirit, I will not faint nor grow weary but I will continue to do good. I have faith [a promise from YOUR Word which is the substance of what I'm hoping for; the tool I need to meet the goal] that I will reap good in due season [rain or snow, summer or winter].

I have a command from YOU to be strong & to be very courageous because I always have YOUR presence with me! So I keep the Book of the Law [the Kingdom of God works by a law of seed time & harvest] in my mouth & I meditate in it day & night observing to do according to all that is written in it. Now, I have the Raw Supernatural power from YOU to get wealth to make my way prosperous, I deal wisely and I have good success, and whatever I put my hand to prospers, in Jesus name!

Lord my God, YOU are my Source, my Family's Source & my friends' Source. The rabbi Paul has already prayed the dynamic heaven moving TRUTH on our behalf that YOU shall supply all our need according to YOUR riches & infinite resources in glory by Christ Jesus

(Messiah Yeshua). The book of Revelation 21:18-19 tells us of jasper, pure gold like pure glass, the foundations of the wall with precious stones of jasper, sapphire, chalcedony, emerald, sardonyx, sardius, chrysolite, beryl, topaz, chrysoprase, jacinth and amethyst; each individual gate is one pearl; the streets pure gold & transparent like glass! Praise YOU Lord that YOU provide for us according to that kind of richness! YOU ARE THE KING OF BLING! The Prince of Life, the King of Glory!

Thank YOU that the Blessing of Adonai, YOU Lord, make me rich & YOU don't mix sorrow with it. I speak with understanding that the Blessing is Your liberalness, Your pool. I am diving into this POOL; I'm going deep in over my head into the Lord from Whom the Blessing flows to me. YOU are the You are the Seed, the Root, & the Vine of the Blessing that is on the life of anyone who would believe they are the seed of Abraham, an heir of God & a joint heir with CHRIST JESUS/YESHUA. Everything the King of Glory has belongs to me on whom, in whom, to whom & through whom the glory whom the glory is being revealed since the GLORY is here!

FASTING & PRAYING

Iam a believer. I do what I know to do because <u>inappropriate & illegal things have to exit</u> my life & some things only by fasting & praying and ALWAYS with EXPECTATION! So, even in the midst of seemingly hopeless situations I turn away from man, my flesh, the factual circumstance, the phone calls, the letters, my senses & symptoms to where I see nothing & nobody but JESUS bringing His reality of the Kingdom of God into the earth for me, putting out His hand giving me and those I'm praying for the touch we need. Above all, my ears and mind are alert & my heart is receptive with confidence that on my account, JESUS HIMSELF said that HE IS WILLING!

I thank my God in heaven in the Name of Jesus that HE will no longer make me wait on HIS performance of His WORD but He is the God Who is Able to change things and is now making crooked places straight IMMEDIATELY! At the confession & profession of His Word that is Truth, the AT ONCE has to happen for me & mine on the Authority of His Name & His Word!

I expect the gifts of the spirit, healing, health, miracles, grace, the threshold of heaven, answered prayer and power to do all things [even more than YOU did on earth according to YOUR word Lord Jesus, so that to YOU I'm a good soldier & have a life that is worth something to the Kingdom]. I also expect to see the tremendous power of heaven on earth, ever increasing faith [especially as I add

to my faith according to 2 Peter 1: 5-8]
and brotherly love [starting with my own
siblings & me]. The ATOMIC POWER
OF GOD via fasting and praying and
even past times of prayers sowed, has & is
opening the windows of these blessing to
me NOW in Jesus' name!

LORD GOD, I seek YOU & YOUR
Kingdom 1st! To YOU I make all my pleas
& commit all my causes! YOU do great &
unsearchable & marvelous things, deeds
beyond investigation, wonders beyond all
reckoning! YOU give rain on the earth &
send/pour water on the field. YOU set on
high those who are lowly, & those who
mourn are lifted to safety. I am happy
that YOU, God correct me and chasten/
discipline me [even by checking me
on the way & the heart condition with
which I think and speak]. YOUR joy,
YOUR Word, is my strength...I LOVE
YOU!!! It feels like a bruise, sores, strikes

and a wound at times, BUT <u>ONLY YOU</u> <u>are able to bandage and bind me back</u> <u>up and it is YOUR hands that heal &</u> <u>make me whole</u>. YOU shall deliver/rescue me in **six** troubles, from six disasters. In **seven,** no harm or evil shall touch me, so I will not be afraid of destruction when it comes. **I shall laugh at destruction and famine!** I shall know that my tent is safe and at peace, I shall visit my dwelling and nothing shall be amiss…looking around my home and miss nothing [even in this I have the promise of having a home of my own, and something in it, GLORY TO GOD]. I shall not die before my time but will come to the grave at full age. In the meantime, I will declare the Wonderful Works of the living Awesome Mighty God.

KINGDOM MINDSET

The wealth of the wicked is coming into my righteous hand for whom it was laid up…AND THIS BY the way the Kingdom of God works—I believe it, I sow it into my spirit, I meditate on the Word-giver of this truth, I abide in Him, I let the Word abide in me, I think it's TRUTH for me, my family & friends, I ask, seek & knock for wisdom which comes from God, I receive the wisdom & the power to get the wealth BY SPEAKING IT & my Father in Heaven will do it for me! It is possible for me because all things are possible to them that believe & I serve the GOD OF POSSIBILITIES…

AGAIN <u>HIS WORD</u> will not return void but ACCOMPLISHES & PROSPERS ONLY!

ADORATION

Lord, You are to me JUST GOOD! MARVELOUS! FAITHFUL! ABLE! FLAWLESS! WORTHY OF MY DEEPEST LOVE, AFFECTION, DEVOTION, CONSECRATION & DEDICATION! YOU are HOLY! RIGHTEOUS & YOU DO RIGHT ONLY! YOU are THE MOST WISE, MOST HIGH, MOST LOVELY, MOST READY TO PERFORM YOUR WORD! I won't let YOU, heaven & the angels wait anymore in anticipation for me to speak YOUR word. I open my mouth Father & thank YOU that the Powerful Holy Spirit fills me up!

DECLARATION & DECREE

It's time for the Harvest! It's time for the Higher Life! It's time for the Higher dimension of living for YOU & living like I'm a citizen & ambassador of a Kingdom that is ruled by a God Who sits on the throne and rests His feet on the earth because He's mighty like that! A God WHO tells the waters to only come to a certain level on the beach & they obey because He's runnin' things like that! The ONE WHO's WORD alone is holding up the sun & the moon & even if they vanish, HIS WORD REMAINS & heaven has it established! The ONE

WHO can merely look at the proud &
bring them low! The ONE WHO gave
the roar to the lion but chose His children,
even His daughter to take dominion over
it!

L. T. Simmons

SCRIPTURE REFERENCES

1) Psalm 46:10
2) 1Corinthians 13: 1
3) 1 Peter 5: 6, 7
4) Psalm 138: 8
5) Romans 3:21-23
6) Matthew 6:33
7) 2 Corinthians 9:7
8) 2 Corinthians 9:8
9) Ephesians 1:18
10) Psalm 35:27
11) Psalm 103:20
12) Genesis 1:2; Luke 1:35
13) Deuteronomy 28:2-4

14) Psalm 23

15) Isaiah 54:17

16) Matthew 14-16-19

17) John 6:63

18) John 15:3-17

19) 2 Thessalonians 3:12-13

20) Joshua 1: 6-8

21) Psalm 1:1-3

22) Genesis 8:22

23) Deuteronomy 8:18

24) Phil 4:19

25) Proverbs 10:22

26) Isaiah 40:4

27) Matthew 8:3, 8

28) Proverbs 13:22

29) Psalm 1:1-2

30) James 1:5

31) Matthew 7:7

32) John 15: 1-3

33) 2 Corinthians 4: 13

34) Jeremiah 1:12

35) Proverbs 8:29

36) Matthew 5:35

37) Genesis 1

38) Psalm 119:89

39) Hebrews 4:16

40) 2Cor 9: 7-10-11

41) Isaiah 55:8-11

42) John 15: 4, 5, 7-8

43) Psalm 139: 23-24

44) Revelation 21:18-19

45) 2 Peter 1: 5-8

46) Job 5:8-11, 17-27

47) Psalm 91:1

BIBLE VERSIONS USED

Amplified

New King James

The Message

ABOUT THE AUTHOR

L.T. Simmons is a young professional trained in the areas of forensics, research and medical science, but has found it imperative to be identified first with Lord Who is ordering her steps every single day. On her journey of life, love, joy, financial excellence, social awareness, and spiritual integrity, her heart has doubled in size with hopes of housing, feeding and encouraging women, children and households wherever there is weariness, confusion, poverty, fear, illness, discouragement or just plain tiredness! The hope is that this book will be translated in several languages so that the love with which it was written will not be limited by borders but be available both nationally and internationally!

The writer truly believes that the JOY of the Lord is our STRENGTH! Again, we are admonished, before battle to be Strong in the Lord and in the power of His might. The author is inviting you to enter a, much deserved strength-inducing rest. As you read, read OUT LOUD and let the Words do the work of strengthening you…transforming you from the inside out.

In the words of a great woman who taught me many things—Stay Encouraged!

www.ingramcontent.com/pod-product-compliance
Lightning Source LLC
Chambersburg PA
CBHW051250120626
46547CB00014B/1885